To Helen and Catherine

JANETTA OTTER-BARRY BOOKS

First published in Great Britain and the USA in 2011 by
Frances Lincoln Children's Books, 4 Torriano Mews,
Torriano Avenue, London NW5 2RZ
www.franceslincoln.com

A catalogue record for this book is available from the British Library.

ISBN 978-1-84780-128-9

Set in Green

Printed in Dongguan, Guangdong, China by Toppan Leefung in October 2010

1 3 5 7 9 8 6 4 2

NEW SHOES
FOR HELEN

Ifeoma Onyefulu

F

FRANCES LINCOLN
CHILDREN'S BOOKS

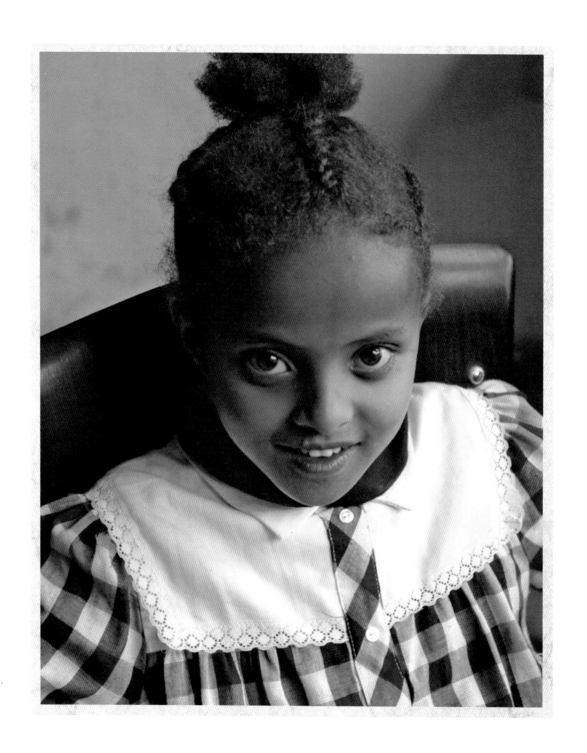

This is Helen Buli.

This is her brother, Nigusu Buli.

Helen needs a new pair of shoes
for her auntie's wedding.

But what kind of shoes
does Helen like?

"Try these on," says Mama, showing
her a pair of shiny red shoes.

Will Helen like the new shoes?

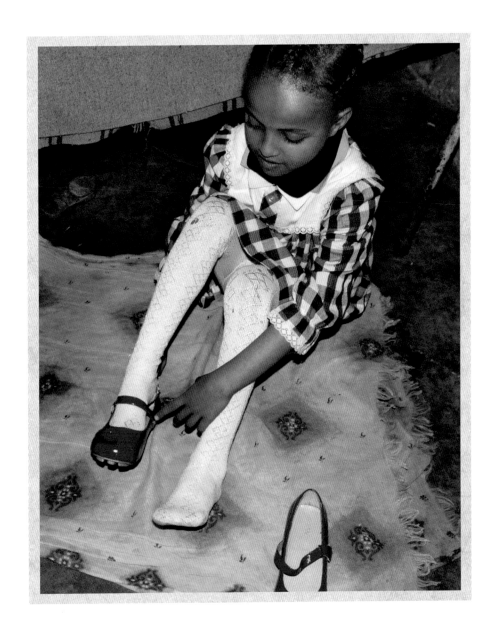

"They're too red, Mama!" says Helen.

Nigusu says, "What about these shoes?
They're nice!"

Will Helen like them?

"They're too small and yellow!" she says.

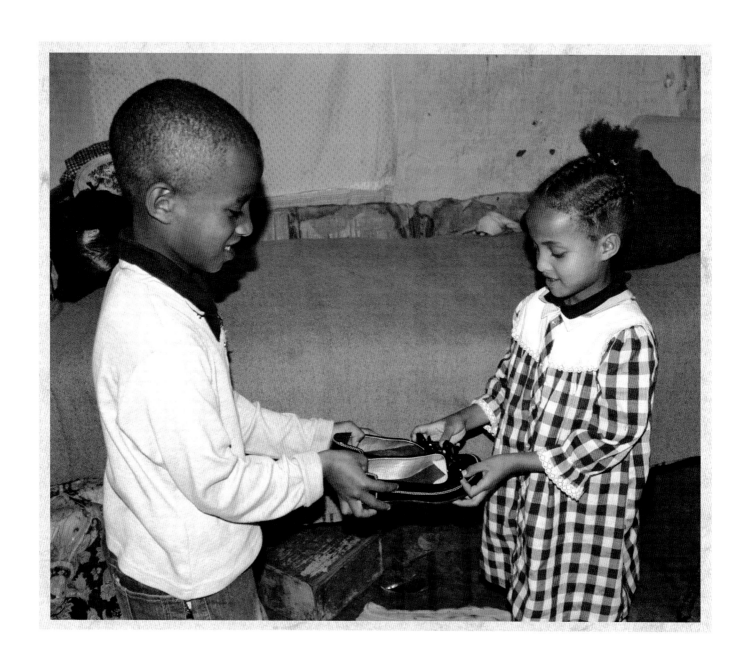

Nigusu shows her another pair.
"They're black and shiny!" he says.

Will Helen like them?

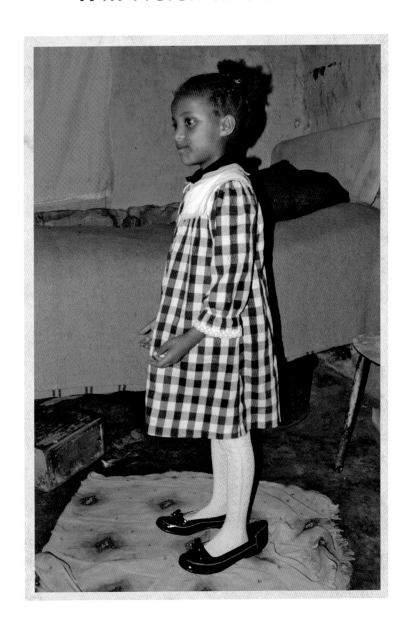

"They're too big, Nigusu!" she says.

"Look at these beautiful shoes!"
says Mama very gently.

Will Helen like them?

"But they're just brown and white,
Mama!" she says.

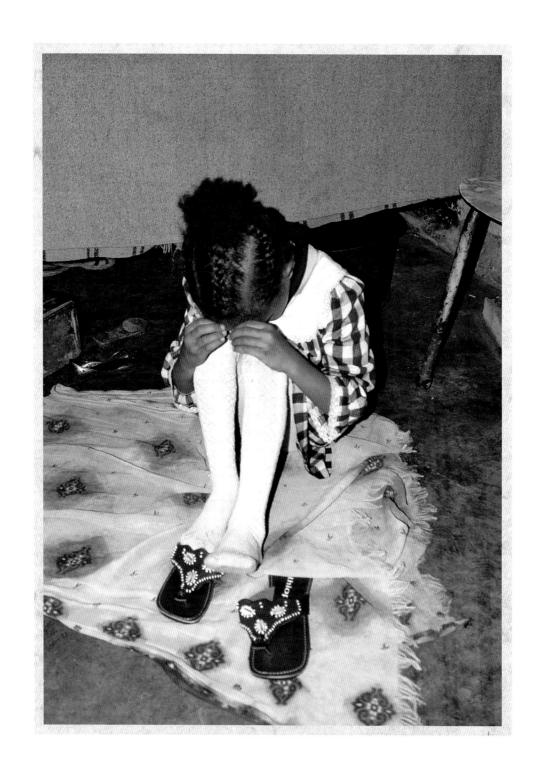

Will Helen ever find the shoes she likes?

Weynishet, who lives next door, offers Mama
a cup of coffee. "Take your daughter to
the market, it's full of shoes," she says.

So Mama, Nigusu and Helen
take a taxi to the market.

They drive past a fruit
and vegetable stall,

and a clothes shop,

until at last they
find the shoe stalls.

"Selam!" says a shoe seller.

"Selam!" says Mama. "Your finest pair
of shoes for my daughter, please!"

"Of course, Madam, I have the best shoes in the whole world!" replies the lady.

She hands Mama a shoebox.

Mama helps Helen try on the shoes.

Will she like a pair of turquoise shoes
with shiny straps?

"They're really beautiful, Mama!" smiles Helen.
Mama smiles too, and pays for them.

Later, Helen shows Papa her new shoes.
"They're really lovely!" he says.

Helen jumps for joy. Helen has new shoes
to go to her first ever wedding. Lucky Helen!

For Every
Individual...

The
INDIANAPOLIS PUBLIC
Library

Renew by Phone
269-5222

Renew on the Web
WITHDRAWN
www.imcpl.org

For General Library Infomation
please call 275-4100